The Adventures of George Washington

By MARGARET DAVIDSON

Pictures by SEYMOUR FLEISHMAN

A hardcover edition of this book is published by Four Winds Press, a division of Scholastic, and is available through your local bookstore or directly from Four Winds Press, 50 West 44th Street, New York, N.Y. 10036.

SCHOLASTIC INC.
New York Toronto London Auckland Sydney

ISBN 0-590-41814-9

12 11 10 9 8 7 6 5 4 3   0 1 2/9

Printed in the U.S.A.   08

Contents

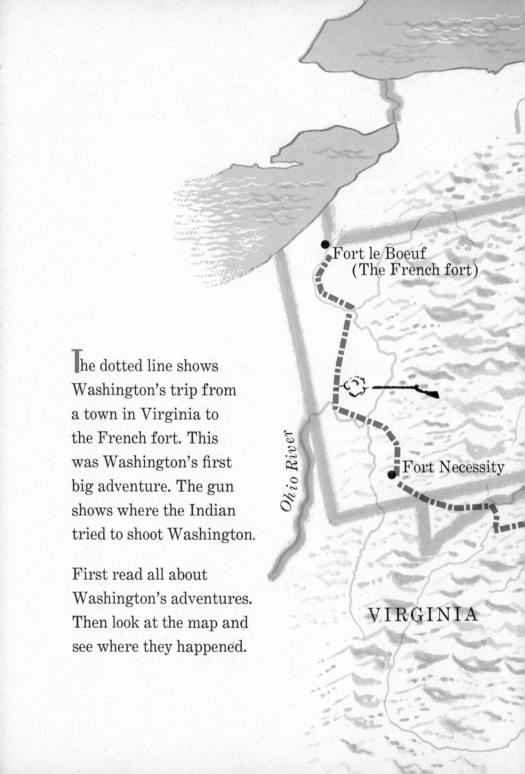

Fort le Boeuf
(The French fort)

The dotted line shows Washington's trip from a town in Virginia to the French fort. This was Washington's first big adventure. The gun shows where the Indian tried to shoot Washington.

First read all about Washington's adventures. Then look at the map and see where they happened.

Ohio River

Fort Necessity

VIRGINIA

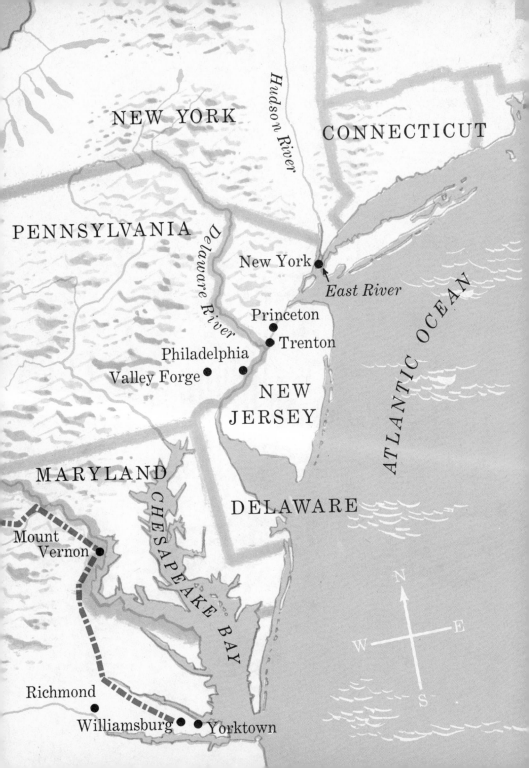

"Get Off My Land"

WHEN GEORGE WASHINGTON was born, there was no United States of America. There were only thirteen colonies. And they all belonged to England.

George Washington was born in the colony of Virginia on February 22, 1732. He was born on a farm. In those days there were no big cities. There weren't many roads. Most people lived on farms.

But as Washington grew up, more and more people came to the colonies. Soon most of the good farm land was gone.

So the people began to move into the lands west of the English colonies. And then there was trouble. Three different groups of people said the western lands belonged to them — the English, the French, and the Indians.

The English king said, "All the land west of our colonies belongs to England too."

But the French king said the land belonged to France.

And the Indians said, "This is our land. Our god gave all this land to us."

Nobody paid any attention to the Indians. And the King of France sent his soldiers to build forts in the wilderness west of Virginia.

When the King of England heard about this, he sent a letter to the Governor of Virginia. This letter was the beginning of George Washington's adventures.

The King wrote, "Tell the French to get off my land."

The Governor couldn't take this letter to the French soldiers. He was too busy. But whom could he send in his place? He wanted someone who was young and strong. Someone who was smart. Someone who could keep his mouth shut and his eyes open.

The Governor had heard of a young man who knew all about the western lands — a man who knew because he had spent three months there, measuring land for farms. In October of 1753, Governor Dinwiddie of Virginia gave twenty-one-year-old George Washington the King's letter.

Washington got on his horse and rode west for several days and nights. Then he came to the beginning of the wilderness — land that now is part of the states of Pennsylvania and Ohio. In Washington's day, this land seemed very far west indeed.

On and on he went. Then he came to land that was strange to him. He needed a guide — someone who knew the land. Washington hired a woodsman named Christopher Gist to guide him to the French.

After many days the men came to the French fort. George Washington gave his letter to the French commander.

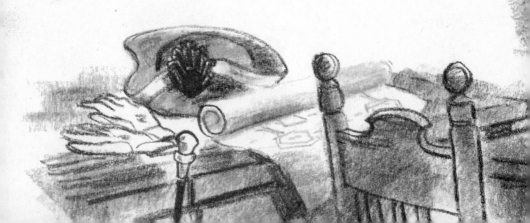

The commander read the letter carefully.
Then he shook his head. "There's nothing I
can do," he said at last. "I have orders to stay."
The French would not leave the western lands.

"Stop!"

THEIR HORSES WERE TOO TIRED to carry Washington and Christopher Gist back to Virginia. So they had to be left at the French fort. The two men would have to walk until they could find fresh horses.

But now it was December and it was very cold. At home in Virginia, Washington had his own horse. He rode everywhere he wanted to go. He was not used to walking in winter woods.

That night the two men slept on the bare ground. When George Washington woke the next morning, his feet were swollen. How they

hurt! But he got up and followed Christopher through the woods once more. Slowly.

Snow began to fall as they went deeper and deeper into the woods. It was very quiet. Washington could not even hear his own footsteps in the soft snow. Christopher Gist looked all around him. He didn't know which way to go. Were they lost?

Suddenly an Indian stepped out from behind a tree. "Follow me," he said. He told the men he would show them the way through the woods. And, the Indian said, the men could sleep in his cabin when night came.

Christopher frowned. He didn't trust the Indian. He knew that many Indians hated the white men who were taking their land. And this Indian was carrying a gun.

But Washington said, "We have to trust

him, Chris. We're lost, and I have to get home quickly."

The two men followed the Indian. But after a time Christopher stopped. The Indian seemed to be leading them *away* from Virginia — not toward it. Christopher asked the Indian, "Where is this cabin of yours? How far away is it?"

The Indian answered. "It is as far away as this — as far as a gun can be heard."

The two men followed again. They walked behind the Indian for a long time. Christopher spoke again, "How far is your cabin now?"

"Two war whoops away," the Indian said.

"Something's wrong," Chris whispered to Washington. "He's not leading us in the right direction at all. It's a trap!"

Then Christopher Gist shouted, "Stop!"

The Indian stopped. He spun around and
fired his gun at the men. Christopher fell to the
ground.

Washington yelled, "Are you hurt?" He
ran over to his friend. Christopher wasn't hurt.
He sat up quickly and aimed his gun at the
Indian. But before Christopher could fire,

Washington knocked the gun out of his hand. "No," he cried, "let him go."

The Indian was gone. But he might come back. It would be easy for him to creep up behind them in the woods.

The sun went down, but Washington and Christopher Gist kept on walking. They walked all night. And they walked the next day too. They wanted to get out of the dark woods. Finally they came to the last trees. Now they stood in the sunlight. They were safe.

"I Heard the Bullets Whistle"

ABOUT FOUR MONTHS LATER, more than a hundred men left the colony of Virginia. Their horses were old. Their guns were older still. They didn't have any uniforms at all. But they were soldiers — off to fight the French. And out in front of them rode George Washington.

He was only twenty-two years old. He didn't know a thing about war. But the Governor

had been watching him. Governor Dinwiddie thought George was a natural leader — someone other men would listen to. So he made George Washington a high officer. *Colonel* George Washington led the first group of soldiers into the western lands.

Washington's men had to cut a road into the wilderness. Step by step, ax blow by ax blow, they cut through the woods. It was hard work. The men became tired. At last Colonel Washington called a halt. They had come to a hill. It would be a good resting place. There was grass for the horses. There was water for the men. Washington told his soldiers to make log buildings and fences. This was the first English fort in the West, and they called it Fort Necessity.

And there Washington and his men waited. One day passed. Then two. The men were getting tired of waiting. They knew the French were somewhere in those woods — but where? Late on the third day an Indian slipped into camp. He came to Washington and said, "I am Silver Heels, one of Half-King's braves. He has sent for you."

Washington nodded. He knew Half-King. Half-King was a friend.

Silver Heels pointed into the forest. "We have seen footprints in the woods. Footprints of French shoes. I will take you to Half-King.

He will show you these footprints and lead you to the French."

Washington and his soldiers followed Silver Heels into the woods. They walked all night before they came to the camp of Half-King. Half-King made a sign with his hand, *follow me.* He led the soldiers back into the woods. Finally he stopped. He pointed. And there, Washington saw the French soldiers hidden under a big cliff. And the French saw George Washington. Suddenly — *peeaaannng* — the the first bullet of the war was fired.

Washington's men were ready for a fight. They had come looking for one. But the French soldiers were surprised. Most of them had been sleeping, and it took time for them to jump up and grab their guns. Too much time. The fight was soon over. And Washington won.

He was very proud. As soon as George Washington got back to Fort Necessity, he sat down and wrote a letter to a friend. He wrote, "I heard the bullets whistle. It was a charming sound."

His friend repeated Washington's words to another man. That man told another. Finally, somebody even told the King of England what George Washington had written. The King smiled. "So bullets sound charming to the young man," he answered. "He would not think so if he had heard many."

Washington and his men lost the next battle. He had to surrender Fort Necessity to the French. Then he went back to Virginia.

But the war went on and on, and a year later, Colonel Washington was back fighting the French and Indians again. He and his men never had enough guns, bullets, food, or blankets. But they went on fighting for three more years. Finally, in the winter of 1758, the last French soldiers had to leave the western woods. The English won the war. And George Washington went home to his plantation, Mount Vernon.

The Quiet Years

WASHINGTON SAT DOWN at his desk. He picked up his pen and wrote a letter to England. "Send me the best blue velvet to make a coat. Send enough for a tall man. Also send fine silk buttons, six pairs of very neat shoes, and six pairs of gloves."

George Washington was getting married. On January 6, 1759, he put on his blue velvet coat and married Martha Custis. Martha had been married before, but her first husband was dead. Now she came to Mount Vernon with her two little children, Jacky and Patsy.

Washington smiled as he led Martha into the big house. He had everything he wanted now. A wife. Two children. And Mount Vernon,

the land he loved so much. The quiet years began.

Each day George Washington got on his horse and rode over his land. And there was a lot of it. For Mount Vernon was really five farms. All the farms together made up the plantation of Mount Vernon. Washington watched his slaves working in the fields. He talked to the many men and women who worked in the shops — weavers, shoemakers, tailors, blacksmiths, carpenters. He watched

Martha work with the cooks and maids in the big house.

And some sunny afternoons he went down to the edge of his land — down to the banks of the Potomac River. For he loved to see his fishermen catch the different kinds of fish that swam in the river. The fish were packed in barrels of salt and sent to England. There they were sold.

Washington had to know everything that went on at Mount Vernon. He had to know when to buy supplies — medicine, seeds, cloth from England. He had to know when to sell his crops. He had to know what was growing in each of his fields. All this took a lot of planning. Sometimes George Washington thought his work would never end.

He worked hard. And he played hard, too.

A fox hunt.... A game of cards in the evening. ...And many parties were given at Mount Vernon. Parties where he danced and danced. Washington loved to dance so much that sometimes he whirled the whole night through — and then rode right off to work in the morning.

So the years passed. Sixteen years. He was forty-three. Washington was growing older,

and he was sure his adventures were behind him now. He didn't miss them at all.

George Washington didn't miss adventure. But adventures were happening all around him. The quiet years were over.

The American colonies had belonged to England for many years. But now many Americans wanted to be free from English rule.

Would there be war? Would the Americans have to fight England? Many people didn't want to fight.

But in March, 1775, a man named Patrick Henry gave a speech in Richmond, Virginia. It was a strong speech. He told the Americans to fight for their freedom. Patrick Henry said, "Give me liberty or give me death." And many people listened.

"Who is That Man in Uniform?"

BUT IF WAR CAME, who would lead the soldiers? Who would be the commander-in-chief? That was the big question now — a question that had to be answered quickly.

Many important men of the colonies met together in the town of Philadelphia to talk about their troubles with England. There were merchants from New York, lawyers from New England. There were men who simply had a lot of money. And a tall planter from Virginia — George Washington.

The roads between Mount Vernon and Philadelphia were soft with spring mud. George Washington was a few days late to the meeting. When he came through the door, everyone looked up. One man turned to another and asked, "Who is that tall man in uniform?" George Washington was so sure war would start soon that he had come dressed in his old army uniform!

Who would make the best general for the new American army? Everyone had his choice. And almost everyone got up and made a speech for the man he wanted. George Washington did not make a speech. He might whisper a word to a friend. But no speeches. He was too shy for that.

Most of the men at the meeting had heard of George Washington. And when the question was asked, "Who do you think is the greatest man here?" the answer came back, "If you mean who can make the best speeches, I'd say Rutledge of South Carolina. But if you want a man of sound judgment, George Washington of Virginia is the greatest man here."

Many must have agreed with this. For on June 15, 1775, the men picked their general — George Washington of Virgina.

Washington wanted this job. Yet at the same time he didn't want it. He remembered too much. He remembered watching men go hungry in that other war so long ago. He remembered watching them die. War was no game of whistling bullets to George Washington now.

But he believed in this fight. He wanted America to be free. And he had to admit to himself that he really did like to be in the middle of things. He liked to lead men. "Just one more adventure," Washington thought to himself.

In the summer of 1775, he said good-bye to Martha. He got on his horse and rode away from Mount Vernon. General George Washington was riding away to the biggest adventure of all — the Revolutionary War.

"Are You the Men I Am
to Defend America With?"

FARMERS AND BACKWOODSMEN, storekeepers and clerks and lawyers — twenty thousand Americans left their homes and marched off down the roads. They were ready to fight.

But they didn't know *how*. Most of them had never been to war before. So they made mistakes at first. And General Washington made mistakes too. It had been seventeen years since he had led men to war. Sometimes he gave the wrong orders. Sometimes he fought battles in the wrong places. And then there came the day when he was almost killed — because he lost his temper.

Washington and his men were in the city of New York. The English army was nearby, looking for a fight.

Very early on the morning of September 15, 1776, five English ships began to move up the East River. At first the Americans didn't see them coming. It was still too dark. But then the sun came up. The day was bright and sunny.

Washington's men could see the English soldiers on the river now. But where would the enemy land?

No one knew. But everyone tried to guess. If General Washington could learn the answer

in time, the American army might win the coming fight.

Small groups of soldiers were moving this way and that. Suddenly the English ships attacked. Eighty English cannon began to roar. Soon the air was so full of smoke that Washington's men couldn't see anything.

But they could hear. And through the smoke came the sound of water lapping against wood, and the sound of oars rowing English soldiers toward the shore. Then the men heard the sound of wood bumping against the stones. And they knew that the boats had landed.

Everything was quiet for a moment, and then came a splashing sound. The English soldiers had climbed over the sides of their boats and were wading ashore now. They came

marching through the city streets — looking
for the American army.

The Americans were so frightened by this
time, they began to run. They didn't even stop
to fire a shot.

When General Washington saw this, his
face became red with anger. He threw his hat
on the ground and cried, "Are you the men I
am to defend America with?" But the men
paid no attention to their general. They were
running too fast.

Washington got madder and madder. He

took out his gun. "You run in every direction but the right one. Get back and fight," he called in warning. But the men still ran. Washington pulled the trigger of his gun. It jammed.

So he threw the gun away and pulled out his sword. The sword swished through the air — but one of his soldiers grabbed it and threw it on the ground. Then Washington took his riding whip and began to beat the men as they ran past his plunging horse. Still they paid no attention. They would not fight.

And the English came closer and closer. Soon they would be upon General Washington. Bullets flew through the air all around him. Just then, one of his officers ran up beside him and grabbed the bridle of his horse. The officer dragged the horse and rider to a safe place.

General Washington was safe. But as they were riding away, the officer heard Washington mutter to himself, "Did you see? I was lost — lost in a sea of men gone rat."

The Old Fox

THE ENGLISH SOLDIERS began to make fun of George Washington. They began to call him the Old Fox. They pretended they were hunters chasing an old fox. And the old fox always ran away.

The English chased Washington's army across the colony of New Jersey. They chased the Americans across the Delaware River into Pennsylvania. And there, on the banks of the river, the Americans stopped running. They were too tired to run any more.

They were cold and hungry. They grumbled to each other. "I don't mind staying if we get a chance to fight. But we don't fight. We've lost this war. It's no use any more. Why not just leave?"

And many of them did leave. When night came, a man would slip out of camp. Then another. Each morning General Washington woke to see his army smaller and smaller.

On December 18, 1776, Washington sat in his tent and wrote these words: *"I think the game is pretty well up."* But then he put down his pen. He wouldn't write, *"We can't win."* He wouldn't quit.

The Old Fox Plays a Trick

WASHINGTON DECIDED to try one more time. He would fight one more battle.

The American army was camped on the west side of the Delaware River. Across the river lay the town of Trenton, New Jersey. Trenton was held by fifteen hundred Hessians — German soldiers who were paid to fight for the English. Washington knew that he could not beat the Hessians if the Hessians knew he was coming. But what if he tricked them? What would happen then?

The Old Fox had a plan.

He waited until Christmas night of 1776. It was a stormy night. The snow was piling up on the ground. General Washington and his men crept out of camp. They made their way down to the river and climbed into some boats. The river was full of ice. But Washington got his army across the water to the other side.

It was very late now. Washington could hear music coming from the town of Trenton. It was Christmas, and a few of the Hessian soldiers were still singing songs. But most of them were asleep. They had eaten a big dinner, drunk a lot of wine. Now they were fast asleep.

Washington attacked. The Hessian soldiers didn't expect a battle that night. They jumped up and tumbled out of their tents. Bullets flew

through the streets of Trenton. The Hessians were sleepy, surprised, and full of wine. Soon they gave up — still dressed in their nightshirts. The town of Trenton belonged to the Americans.

General Washington had won an important battle. But the war wasn't over yet. The English were angry when they heard about Trenton. A big English army came marching, marching across New Jersey to take Trenton back.

On January 2, 1777, the English General Cornwallis led his five thousand soldiers up to the town. And there was Washington's little army, trapped in the town of Trenton.

It was late in the evening. "We've got him now!" General Cornwallis crowed. And he sent his men to bed. "We'll bag the Old Fox in the morning. He can't get away now."

But Washington had one more trick to play. During the night, the English campfires burned high. The American fires burned higher still. When the English saw these big fires, they thought that the Americans were trying to keep warm.

It was another trick.

During the night, the whole American army crept away into the woods. They left the great fires burning behind them.

It was snowing again, and some of the men had no shoes. Their bare feet left drops of blood in the snow. But they kept on until they left the town of Trenton far behind. It was daylight when the American army reached the town of Princeton, New Jersey — ten miles away from Trenton.

Most of the English soldiers were back at Trenton. But some English were in Princeton. Washington turned to his men. They had taken Trenton. Why not take Princeton too? The battle of Princeton began.

Back in Trenton, General Cornwallis was just getting out of bed when he heard something that sounded like thunder. But the sky was clear. He called to one of his men, "Is that thunder I hear?"

The man listened. He looked toward the

American camp. Empty! "That's not thunder," he yelled. "That's the American army! That's Washington's guns on Princeton!"

General Cornwallis turned his army around and raced toward Princeton. But he was too late. The Americans won there too. And as he chased the last Englishman out of Princeton, George Washington called out, "You wanted to chase a fox. But who is the fox now?"

"Your Country Needs You"

AS THE YEAR 1777 BEGAN, Washington faced a new trouble. Most of the soldiers had signed up to fight for two years. Those years were now up. And the men wanted to go home. They felt that they had done their job. Now it was somebody else's turn.

But Washington knew he could not get a new group of soldiers together before spring. And spring would be too late. Without these men the war would be lost. He must not let them go. General Washington called a meeting of his men.

The drums rolled. The bugles played. And Washington began to talk to the men who were lined up in front of him. He asked them to stay. He promised to pay them more money.

When he was through talking, General Washington rode a little distance away. An officer came before the silent men. "Those who will stay, please step forward," he asked. Drums rolled again. The bugle played. But no one moved! Not one man stepped forward.

Washington couldn't believe it. Was this the answer? Did these men care so little for their country? No! He wouldn't believe it. He would try another time. He rode forward again.

"My brave fellows," he began, "you have done all I asked you to do, and more. But your country is at stake — your wives, your houses, and all you hold dear. You have worn your-

selves out. But we know not how to spare you now. If you will stay," General Washington stopped and cleared his throat, "you can save the cause of liberty."

He turned his horse and rode away slowly. He could not say another word. Tears were rolling down his face. The drums rolled. The bugles played.

The soldiers looked at their general, sitting so quietly on his horse. They looked at one another. And each man had a question in his eyes: "What are *you* going to do?" It was very quiet. And no one moved. Until one man slowly stepped forward. A great sigh came from the line of men. Another man came forward. And then more. Soon most of the men had stepped into the forward line. They would stay. Washington had saved the Revolutionary army.

A Place Called Valley Forge

THE ARMY WAS SAVED, but that was a bad year – 1777. Battles were fought. And battles were lost. Washington's soldiers could not seem to win anywhere. Many men were wounded. Others became ill. They needed everything from bullets to blankets. It was a bad year all around. And the worst of it was the winter – at a place called Valley Forge.

A week before Christmas, the army settled down on the high, windy hill of Valley Forge, Pennsylvania. They would camp there during the winter months. The men had to sleep on

the ground while they built their log huts. But finally the huts were done and the men huddled inside of them. They huddled, and thought of food.

The English army was camped nearby. It

was hard to get food past them and into the American camp. There were days when Washington's men had nothing at all to eat. After a month or two of living at Valley Forge, one soldier wrote home, "All we have to be thankful for is that we are alive and not in the grave with so many of our friends."

The men were cold. They were hungry. And they didn't *have* to shiver through the winter of Valley Forge. They didn't *have* to starve. What was to stop them from going home, where they could warm themselves before their own fires, eat their own food? They could run away.

As January turned into February, and the cold grew worse, Washington was sure this would happen. He was sure his men would leave him now. And he didn't have the heart to blame them if they did.

But he guessed wrong. These men had fought with General Washington for a long time. They had a special feeling for him now. It was partly respect, partly trust — this feeling the men had. He was their leader. They would stay with him.

They were a tiny, half-starved, almost naked army. "But just wait and see," the men said over and over. "One day our luck will change." And they were right. For on the last day of April a messenger rode into camp. "Where's General Washington?" he called out. "I have a letter for him."

Washington read the letter. Then he read it again. When he looked up, his eyes were bright with tears. "We have a powerful friend," he said.

The letter was from the King of France. The King had decided to help the American army. France would send ships and men to help beat back the English. A shout went up into the warm air. "Long live the King of France!" cried Washington's men. Spring had come at last to Valley Forge.

"It Is Done—Well Done"

THAT WAS THE TURNING POINT—when the French came to help the Americans. But it wasn't the end of war. The English fought on. And they were still very strong. They won many more battles in the next two years. But they never caught the Old Fox. For three more years they won most of the battles, but they couldn't win the war.

Then it was the summer of 1781. And the last battle of the war was about to be fought.

Washington was camped outside the city of New York when he got a message from the

French Admiral de Grasse. The Admiral had twenty-nine warships and three thousand men under his command. Would General Washington like to borrow these men and ships?

General Washington wanted this French help. It was the answer to his prayers.

But he still had problems to solve. Where was the English army? That was his first problem — to find the English soldiers. A few of them were in New York City. But most of the English were somewhere else. Where? Finally Washington heard that Cornwallis and his men were camped in the city of Yorktown, Virginia.

So Washington sent a message to the French Admiral de Grasse. He wanted the French ships and soldiers to meet him at Yorktown.

Then General Washington began to make

plans to leave New York. Secretly. For he didn't want those few English soldiers in the city to know he was leaving. If they found out, they might warn Cornwallis at Yorktown.

No, Washington would have to sneak away. He would have to trick the English again.

First he had his men build big ovens — ovens for baking bread. Near the ovens, Washington's men also built many sleeping huts. The English in New York could see the ovens and sleeping huts. This made them think Washington's army was settling down. They thought the Americans were making a camp near New York for the coming winter.

Washington had one more trick to play. He sat down and wrote a letter. In the letter he said that his men were tired. The American army had no plans for fighting. They would

rest at New York. And the English read that letter — for Washington made sure an English spy got hold of it.

Then one night Washington's men let the fires die in the bread ovens. The men left their new huts and crept away. And the English didn't see a thing! Not for two whole days. Then they noticed.

They found the cold bread ovens and the

empty huts. Now they knew that the letter had been a trick. But it was two days too late for the English — Washington's army was far down the road to Yorktown.

Washington had one more worry. Would the French ships and men be at Yorktown when he got there? If the French didn't come, Washington would lose the battle. For Yorktown was right on the Chesapeake Bay. If the French ships didn't come, the English could escape by sea.

Each day Washington hoped to hear from the French Admiral de Grasse. But no message came. Finally, when the American army was very close to Yorktown, Washington saw a horse and rider galloping up the road. The messenger at last!

"Give it to me," Washington commanded. He opened the letter. Thank God! Admiral de Grasse and his ships were at the mouth of the Chesapeake Bay. The trap was set.

The English army was trapped. The French closed in on the sea side. The Americans closed in on land. The English didn't have a chance. On October 18, 1781, their guns stopped. The English surrendered at Yorktown.

The English soldiers marched out of Yorktown. They laid down their guns in front of General Washington. Washington looked up at the new American flag flying over the town. "It is done," he whispered to himself. "It is well done."

The Adventure
He Did Not Want

GENERAL WASHINGTON stayed with his army for two more years. But no more battles were fought. And on December 2, 1783, the last English soldier sailed away from the United States of America.

Now George Washington rode back to Mount Vernon. He was happy. For surely he'd had his last adventure. What more could America want with him?

But the new states weren't getting on with one another very well. Many states were printing their own money. Each state was making its own laws. Each state was beginning to act as a separate country.

The leading men of America said that this must not go on. They met in Philadelphia. There they formed a new kind of government — a stronger central government. It would make some laws for all the states. It would print money for the entire country. The central government would be stronger than any one state.

But the new central government couldn't run itself. It had to have a leader. Americans looked toward Mount Vernon again.

George Washington was very upset. He didn't want this new job. He felt that he had done enough. He was fifty-six years old now. His hair was white. He couldn't see very well without glasses. He had to wear a set of false teeth that pinched his mouth.

He was in his fifties. But the war had made

him feel even older. Now he had a right to stay at Mount Vernon and be a planter again. He had a right to rest.

But many people felt he was the only man who could keep the states working together. Washington was not sure this was true. Still, he gave in and took the job. In 1789 he became the first President of the United States.

But as he rode away from home again, Washington turned to Martha. "Why," he wondered, "do all the roads have to lead *away* from Mount Vernon?" George Washington was riding off to his last adventure — the adventure he did not want.

George Washington was President for eight years. Eight unhappy years. Too many people watched his every move, and that made him nervous. If he wore an old coat, they said he was dressing poor. If he wore a new coat, they said he was playing rich. Finally Washington said to a friend, "I always knew I couldn't please everyone. But can't I please *anyone?*"

And when he had to decide anything, he couldn't look back to what other Presidents had done. He was the first President, and everything was new. It was a hard job, being President in those first years.

But during those eight years the country grew stronger. Finally Washington felt the country was strong enough to do without him. Someone else could take over now. His job was done.

The people were calling Washington the father of his country. And many of them wanted him to be President for four more years. But this time George Washington said *no*. And he meant it. In 1797, he went home to Mount Vernon for the last time.

"Our Dancing Days
Are Over"

A FEW MONTHS after Washington returned to Mount Vernon, he received a letter from a friend. The friend invited George and Martha Washington to come to a dance. Washington loved to dance. Once, in the days long ago, he had been able to dance all night — and go to work in the morning. But now he picked up his pen and answered his friend, "Martha and I thank you," he wrote, "but our dancing days are over."

He was sixty-five. His life had been full of

adventures — some good, some bad. George Washington was not old yet. But he was a very tired man.

For three more years he farmed at Mount Vernon. Then one snowy day in 1799, he got on his horse and rode across the fields. When he returned home that evening, his coat was wet. "Go up and change," Martha begged. But Washington just answered, "No. I'll eat dinner first." The next day he began to feel bad. He had caught cold in the snow, and he was too tired to shake off a cold. He grew weaker and weaker.

The doctor couldn't help. George Washington tossed and turned in his bed for days. Finally the time came when he turned to Martha and said, "I die hard. But I am not afraid to go."

Good-bye

ON DECEMBER 14, 1799, George Washington died at Mount Vernon. When the American people heard that he was dead, they didn't know what to say. He had meant so much to them, done so much for them. How could they find words to describe how they felt about George Washington? How could they say good-bye?

Then an old friend of Washington's found the words. His name was Henry Lee. Mr. Lee stood up in the pulpit of a big church. Many people had gathered there to honor George Washington. For a moment everyone sat in silence. Then Mr. Lee began to speak about George Washington, "First in war," he said, "first in peace, and first in the hearts of his countrymen...."